Seoul, South Korea in 3 Days:

The Definitive Tourist Guide Book That Helps You Travel Smart and Save Time

Finest City Guides

Book Description

Seoul is unique. It has traditional Asian aspects, but many aspects are among the most modern in the world. There is a great deal of contrast in the different areas of Seoul.

The people of Seoul are beautiful and welcoming. Korea is a fashion trendsetter. You can celebrate the authenticity of traditional Korea and still enjoy the technological advantages offered there.

Korea was ravaged by war, that's true. But it has been rebuilt into a thriving economic stronghold that has many influences on the world at large. From modern Korean pop culture to ancient houses of worship, Seoul mixes traditional and modern life in a unique and vibrant atmosphere.

If you only have a few days to spend in Seoul, you need to make the most of them. That's what this travel guide is all about.

Seoul and its home country of South Korea may shape your world view. Theirs is a story of courage and hope, of rebuilding from nothing, and of the undying spirit of the people of South Korea.

The People of Seoul

The population density in Seoul is nearly twice that in New York City! Most residents of Seoul are Korean, with pockets of Japanese, Chinese and minorities of expatriates. The population is over 10 million. The population of Seoul has been decreasing since the 1990's, since it is an aging one, and the costs of living are high.

The people of Seoul tend to be warm and welcoming, and tolerant of tourists who don't quite know where they're going. That's helpful for travelers.

Language

Koreans speak... well, Korean. If you learn a few often-used words, it will be helpful for you. The language, however, is quite different from Western languages, in pronunciation and grammar.

Different areas of Korea speak different dialects, but many people in Seoul speak standard Korean. This makes it a bit easier to communicate in the city, since you'll be hearing predominantly the same dialect.

Korean writing utilizes a phonetic system known as hangul. In this system, sounds are "stacked" into blocks that are representative of syllables. A committee designed the system, and although it looks like small circles and right angles, it's actually logical and consistent. You may find that you can pick it up quite easily.

Religious Beliefs

In Seoul, the two main religions are Buddhism and Christianity. There are smatterings of other religions too, including Confucianism and Muism. Seoul has the largest Christian congregation in the world, at Yoido Full Gospel Church.

Here is a quick preview of what you will learn in this tourist guide:

- Helpful information about Seoul, South Korea
- Flying into the city
- Transportation tips while you're in town
- Why Seoul is such a diverse tourist spot and what you will find most remarkable about it
- Information on luxury and budget accommodations and what you'll get for your money
- The currency used in Seoul
- Tourist attractions you should make time to see
- Other attractions for entertainment and culture
- Events that may be running during your stay
- Tips on the best places to eat & drink for all price points, whether you want simple fare, worldwide dishes or Korean/Asian flavor

Table of Contents

1. Introduction

Seoul is such a diverse city that one can hardly describe it in a short introduction. You'll find much of the old world and much new technology, and there is literally something for everyone.

A Brief History of Seoul, South Korea

Seoul sits on the Han River, and its history goes back more than 2000 years. It was the capital of Korea during some past dynasties. It includes five sites that have been declared UNESCO World Heritage Sites:

- Namhansanseong
- Jongmyo Shrine
- Royal Tombs of the Joseon Dynasty
- Hwaseong Fortress
- Changdeok Palace

Modern Seoul landmarks include the Dongdaemun Design Plaza, the 63 Building, the N Seoul Tower and Lotte World. Lotte World is the second largest indoor theme park in the world. More than 10 million people from all over the world visited Seoul in 2014.

Seoul today is a leading global city, and the fourth largest global metropolitan economy. It has been rated as the most livable city in Asia, and Aradis proclaimed it the city with the second highest global quality of life.

What does Seoul Offer its Visitors?

Since Seoul is the epicenter of more than 5,000 years of history in Korea, you can find remains from ancient Korean civilization. This is an amazing feat, since there have also been two Japanese invasions in Korea, and the Korean War.

You can also find the newest of technology in Seoul. They are on the cutting edge of the newest aspects of technology. Most Koreans seem poised for the future, perhaps since their past was so painful. You'll see signs everywhere proclaiming "New", and that's one way to tell that the people of Korea impatiently await the future. They want everything faster-faster ("pali-pali").

2. Key Information about Seoul, South Korea

Money Matters

The official currency of South Korea is the South Korean Won, or KRW.

The denominations of notes are:
1,000, 5,000 and 10,000 KRW.

The denominations of coins are:
10, 50, 100 & 500 KRW

You can usually get favorable exchange rates in South Korea, since the banks want to market the Korean exchange rates. You may choose to exchange currency at the airport, but visiting a Foreign Exchange Bureau will usually give you a better rate on the exchange.

Tipping

South Korea has a culture that does not involve tipping. No one expects rewards, and this includes staff in restaurants, and even cab drivers. Bellboys and porters similarly do not expect tips.

3. Transport to and in Seoul, South Korea

Getting to Seoul by Plane

It's quite simple to get to Seoul by airplane. The baggage claim and immigration at Incheon International Airport are among the fastest you'll ever see. If you happen to catch a slow time, you can literally be off your plane and on your way to downtown Seoul in 10 minutes.

Getting to Seoul from the Airport

Outside the airport building are buses that can take you straight to Seoul. There are standard and deluxe KAL buses. The deluxe buses cost $6.46 USD for children and $13 USD per adult. The standard buses are $4.31 USD for each child and $7.76 USD for each adult.

Purchase your tickets at the airport unless you have cash. Cash can be used to purchase tickets after you have already boarded a bus. It takes about 45 minutes to get from the airport to Seoul, unless the traffic is heavy. In rush hour, it can easily take twice that long.

Standard taxis cost roughly $52 USD to get to town, and deluxe taxis cost at least $86 USD to get to the downtown area.

The other easy way to get from the airport and Seoul proper is by taking the AREX train, found inside the airport itself. Express tickets can be purchased at the airport, and express trains will drop you right at the downtown Seoul Station.

Seoul Cabs

There are many taxis in Seoul, and it's pretty easy to hail one, unless it's late on a Friday or Saturday night. The fares for taxi service are high, since the rates paid by drivers for gas are so expensive in Seoul.

Many local taxi drivers do not speak much English. They've heard every mispronunciation of local areas enough that they can sometimes figure out where you're heading. Instead of taking chances, just write down your destination in Korean on a piece of paper. In addition, most cabs have GPS units, so drivers can find most places if you have a phone number for the location.

Public Transport in Seoul

Seoul offers you efficient and modern public transportation systems, including buses and subway trains.

Subways

Nine subway lines run through the city and suburbs. The trains are clean, and arrive every five to 10 minutes. The signs are in English, as well as Korean, which makes the subways less daunting.

If you're planning on using the subway, keep these facts in mind:

- The subway is quite popular, since it avoids traffic on the streets. The trains are full in peak travel hours. Try the last cars for a better chance to get a seat.
- Seoul subway fares cost $1.00 - $2.00 USD. You can buy tickets in the stations. The ticket machines have English instructions. Prepaid transit cards are better to use if you want to save money. You can buy the most often used "T-money" card at convenience stores and subway station ticket windows. T-money cards cost $2.16 USD and you can recharge them as needed.

- Carry a map of the subway (available at tourist offices) and check it out before you board. Take note of any transfers you'll be making. Subway lines are coded by color.
- Must subway cars have specially designated seats for those who are disabled, elderly or pregnant.
- Voice announcements for upcoming stations are in English, as well as Korean. Some also are read in Japanese and Chinese.

Buses

Seoul has four color-coded bus categories. The colors are yellow, red, green and blue. The numbers on buses indicate their designated districts, so you can tell where they're going.

The T-card mentioned above is the easiest and cheapest way to pay for bus rides.

City Pass Seoul

This is somewhat like the T-card, but it will also allow tourists to access city tour buses that will take you around the palaces and downtown area. With the City Pass, you can get on and off the tour buses whenever you like, and as many times as you'd like.

Accommodations

Luxury Hotels in Seoul

Seoul has more than 90 luxury hotels. The rates run from $300 per night to over $400 per night.

The Seoul Plaza - $300 USD per night and up

The Seoul Plaza offers the look of a boutique hotel, after its recent expensive and expansive renovation. It shows off a dramatic and modern look.

The Plaza is a great place to stay if you're a first-time Seoul visitor. It is close to the subway and many traditional sights, like museums and palaces. It's also conveniently located with easy access to the Myeong-dong shopping district.

The Shilla – From $300 USD per night and up

From the perch atop a hill, this hotel has a sweeping driveway and a traditional Korean roof. It also has parking for its guests, which is unusual in Seoul, especially since it has a prime downtown location.

The personality of The Shilla shows through the parkland and its 450+ rooms. Society weddings are held here quite often, so you may see paparazzi hordes on weekends. They have a duty-free store next to the hotel building, and it's considered to be the best such store in Seoul. It carries all the latest luxury goods.

The Westin Chosun – from $420 USD per night

Many urban hotels in Seoul feature shiny, sleek, modern architecture. The Westin Chosun reminds one of traditional Korean luxury hotels. The interior design and pavilion are quite reminiscent of the traditional window frames and ceilings in Korea.

That's not what the Chosun is best known for, though – that would be its food. The first French restaurant in Korea is the 9th Gate Grill, in the hotel lobby. It once catered to formal diners, but recently has become a more casual and friendly dining experience.

The Westin Chosun has a prime location, close to markets and the Lotte department store. The rooms are luxurious and the bathrooms are spacious.

Mid-Range Hotels in Hong Kong

The middle range in hotel prices doesn't mean you'll lose some of the favorite amenities available in town. The prices range from $200 USD to $360+ USD

Hotel Skypark Central Myeongdong – from $229 USD per night

Just steps from the Myeongdong Nanta Theatre, Myeongdong Theater and T.um SK Telecom Technology Museum, the Hotel Skypark offers luxury amenities at mid-range prices.

The Hotel Skypark offer travelers a rooftop terrace, restaurant and 24-hour business center. They are happy to help you with assistance with tickets or tours, and the rooms have all the amenities you could want.

Grand InterContinental Seoul Parnas – from $230 USD per night

You may never have received the type of service offered by the Grand InterContinental before, even if you routinely stay at luxury hotels. The concierges will anticipate and fulfill all your needs.

The food at the Grand InterContinental is delicious, and the service is impeccable. For a few extra dollars, you can access the club lounge, which opens up even more doors to delicious foods and hearty drink.

Hilton Millennium Seoul – from $365 USD per night

The Millennium in Seoul offers you style and comfort, in one of the most convenient locations in the area. Relax in one of their newly-renovated mountain view, deluxe rooms or select an executive room, which gives you access to two business lounges with evening cocktails, exquisite views and complimentary breakfast.

You'll earn rewards with the Hilton HHonors program, offering airline miles as well as hotel comps. You'll be in the center of the shopping and business districts. Enjoy a meal in one of their five restaurants or the deli, or grab a drink at the bar.

Seoul Hotels for the Budget-Conscious

You don't need to spend an arm and a leg to stay comfortably in Seoul. Their budget hotels still offer nice rooms and amenities. Rates run from $30 USD to $150 USD per night.

Motel Kakao – from $30 USD per night

You probably won't find a less expensive place to lay your head for the night when you're traveling in Seoul. Perhaps you'd rather spend more money on tours or the duty-free stores than on lodging, in which case a hotel at this price will fit right into your itinerary.

The Morel Kakao is just a bit over 1,000 feet from the Shingil subway station and about two miles from the popular Yeouido Han River Park. They are 50 minutes driving from the airport and 10 minutes driving from the Assembly.

K-haus Dongdaemun – from $46 USD per night

This budget hotel has a handy location, close to Changdeok Palace, Changgyeonggung Palace, Korea University, Dongdaemun Market and the Dongmyo Shrine.

They offer free concierge services to help you plan tours and itineraries, along with express check-in and a 24-hour front desk. They even have multi-lingual staff, which can be quite helpful.

Hotel Gaeul – from $125 USD per night

Hotel Gaeul has a great location, just 800 feet from the Shinchon Subway Station, and seven minutes from entertainment and dining options near Shinchon Ewha Women's University Street. The airport is just a 40-minute drive from the door.

The contemporary styled rooms have 2 PCs for computer access and free Wi-Fi. They were renovated in 2012. With a 24-hour front desk, they offer photocopying and fax services and baggage storage. They even offer free private parking for guests, on the premises.

Airbnb's

The average cost at the Airbnb website for facilities in Seoul is $62 USD per night, but many are lower than this. The price is higher for full-home rentals. There are more than 250 Airbnb spots in Seoul, South Korea.

The Airbnb is a totally different experience as compared to staying in a hotel. Your hosts are usually friendly and helpful, without hundreds of other visitors begging for their attention. You can find locations close to Seoul, and also within easy walking or driving distance to grocery stores, restaurants and even hiking trails in some locations.

4. Sightseeing

Here, we'll suggest the places you just have to see, even if you're only in Seoul for a few days. You could spend much more time in Seoul with so much to do, but these attractions are the places that most people say were the most interesting and inspiring to visit.

The National Museum of Korea

The National Museum is the flagship museum of the art and history of Korea. Its cultural organization represents the country. Established in 1945, the museum is committed to researching and studies in art, archaeology and history, and they offer various education programs and exhibitions.

By 2012, after a 2005 relocation to the Yongsan District, statistics reported that 20 million people have visited the museum. It is consistently among the favorites in activities in Seoul, and it stands as one of the larger Asian museums.

N Seoul Tower

Seoul Tower was opened in 1980, and has been a major tourist attraction ever since. It sits atop Namsan Mountain and gives visitors panoramic views of the city of Seoul and its surrounding areas.

The "N" in the name refers to the New look of the tower, after an expensive renovation in 2005. The color scheme was changed and a newer lighting system was installed. The tower can now be decorated with colored lights for specific events or seasons.

Stop by the N Grill if you're hungry. This revolving, Western style restaurant is very popular among visitors. The views are beyond that which you can find at nearly any other location.

Nam Mountain

At its peak, Nam Mountain is 860 feet in height. The full name in the past was actually Mongmyeoksan, but now it is often called Mt. Namsan. You'll find striking views of the skyline of Seoul, as well as picnic and hiking areas. The N Seoul Tower is found atop Nam Mountain.

The area around the peak is a public park called Namsan Park. It is well-maintained by the Seoul government. There is a smoke signal station on the mountain, as well. Beacon Tower was an integral part of emergency communications in Seoul until 1985.

5. Eat & Drink

One word is used consistently to describe Seoul: fast. In addition to fast Internet speeds and fast construction, they also have fast food, of course. Seoul has millions of residents and visitors, and dining trends may catch like wildfire to dry timber.

Restaurants that receive a lot of hype may have lines of people waiting around the entire block, as people are eager to see what the hype is about. The same restaurants could be closed by the next month. Seoul residents try new things and then move on, if they're not as good as expected.

There is a lot of experimentation in restaurants of Seoul, and many unusual dishes. Even the more conventional restaurants have made improvements, to keep people coming back. They use higher quality ingredients and better methods of food preparation.

If you want to taste all of Seoul, you need to balance the classics like mung bean pancakes and short ribs with newer concoctions, like whipped cream on top of your beer. Really? Yes!

The Seoul restaurants in our guide are classified into three price points:

Expensive Prices (over $42 USD)
Moderate Prices ($15 USD to $30 USD)
Inexpensive Prices (under $15 USD)

Jungsik - Expensive

The media locally and overseas calls the chef here, Jung-sik Yim, the new king of cuisine in Korea. He runs a very tight ship, both here and at his Manhattan restaurant. Everything is exact, from the bible-thick wine list to the plating of dishes like pickled gomchwi and pork belly. Most people dine in coursed tastings, and it's a good idea to get a reservation.

4 & 5 course dinners include everything from tuna and octopus to duck and filet mignon. The 4 course dinner is $77 USD per person and the 5 course meal is $103 USD per person.

OKitchen 3 – Expensive

OK3 specializes in Italian food. The chef worked in Italy for two years, and they even age their own steak and salami. They use freshly picked, local Korean ingredients in unique and clever ways.

The chef, Susumu-san, brings in fresh vegetables and herbs from his private farm. The prices are a bit more reasonable than you might expect, for such an upscale dining experience. Prices for dinners start at $60 USD.

Hadongkwan – Expensive

This restaurant has undergone an extensive renovation, but the original wooden tables and doors are still in use. This helped them to keep the long-time customers happy, since they saw the renovation as losing a landmark.

The signature dish here is gomtang, which is simmered beef soup and rice. If you're mentally or physically tired, you'll find this to be a wonderful comfort food. It includes plenty of rice and beef pieces, made with Korean beef. They even serve it in the most traditional of Korean bowls, made from bronzeware. Prices start at $43 USD.

Moderately Priced Restaurants

Spacca Napoli – Moderate

Using a wood oven, Spacca Napoli offers some of the best pizza in Seoul. The wood taste makes the pizza unique and still traditional in flavor. There are lots of Italian restaurants where you can dine in Seoul, but this restaurant offers the real taste of Italy, for $10-$30 USD.

Wansangol Myungga Apgujeong 2 – Moderate

The Wansangol Myungga Apgujeong 2 offers one of Korea's favorite foods, bibimbap. This tasty dish is served at many Korean restaurants, but arguably done better here than anywhere else. The food is basically soup with vegetables and bean sprouts.

The staff at the Wansangol Myungga Apgujeong uses only pure ingredients, in creating healthy dishes. The staff is friendly and the prices are reasonable, from $10-$30 USD.

3 Alley Seoul – Moderate

This is a clean, new-looking pub-style restaurant, and even has big screen TVs. Their Aussie burger is very popular, including Aussie beef with beetroot.

While you enjoy sporting events on the big screens, try a side of potato wedges. They are crispy and well-seasoned, and they come with sweet chili sauce and sour cream. They also offer many imported beers. Prices range from $20-$28 USD.

Inexpensive Restaurants

Jyoti Restaurant – Inexpensive

Indian food is popular in Seoul, and Jyoti is one of the best places to get it. The dishes are tasty and well-presented and they have abundant portions. They have set lunch menus, with a good variety of dishes and attractive prices.

Even for dinner, the prices are low, and you get a lot of food for the money. Make no mistake, it's also GOOD food. The most recommended dishes are chicken tandoori and chicken butter marsala. Prices range from $7-$12 USD.

Bao – Inexpensive

This casual restaurant has many food choices, and you get to build your own meals. Starting with carbs like noodles and rice, you will add a protein (including tofu as a choice) and then extra touches like coriander and cashews. You will also be choosing your flavor palette, from Malay, Thai and Chinese.

The side dishes at Bao are tasty, as well. The calamari is a favorite. This is a relaxed place to eat dinner in the middle of a bustling area. Prices range from $7-$13 USD

Brew 3.14 - Inexpensive

Microbrews and fried chicken are a couple of the favorites on the Brew 3.14 menu. You can speak with people from all over the world as you enjoy your meal. The atmosphere is laid back, so it won't intimidate travelers. Chicken and pizza are the specialties; no veggie and rice dishes are served.

Travelers recommend the spicy chicken balls, if you happen to be an adventurous diner. This is an intimate restaurant, perfect for a quick bite for two to four people. The prices range from $6-15 USD.

Culture and Entertainment

Seoul, South Korea has a diversity unlike many cities. The past and the present – and the future – all coexist in harmony. You can tour ancient palaces and then visit modern shopping districts and amusement parks. Driving everything is a business and technological-oriented society.

In Seoul, the urban and natural landscapes mingle. Even while biking in Han River Park, you will never escape the apartment complexes and looming skyscrapers of Seoul. You will learn to appreciate the different types of beauty found here.

The city planners in Seoul molded the city landscape purposefully so that the old and new would be well-balanced. The city does not show random progress, but rather years of planning. The culture, too, is becoming more multifaceted.

Just as you leave a shining skyscraper, your ears may be beckoned by the voices of native Korean song and the beating of drums. You can find Koreans singing and dancing in traditional clothing, even as you are marveling at Seoul's technology.

The nature, the buildings, the neon lights and the people all merge into something that will become more comfortable as you spend a few days in Korea. Seoul today is a bit of a cultural chimera, but in their fast-fast world, it works.

Gyeongbokgung Palace

This amazing palace was built in 1395, and is commonly called the Northern Palace. It was nearly destroyed once by fire in the Japanese invasions between 1592 and 1598, but all the buildings of the palace have been painstakingly rebuilt.

Most original edifices remained more or less intact, and the sculptures in the Royal Audience Chamber are representative of past contemporary art sculptures.

Bongeunsa Temple

This Buddhist temple was founded in 794, and sits on a Sudo Mountain slope. Buddhism was repressed severely in the Joseon Dynasty, but this temple was rebuilt under the rule of a Queen in that dynasty. Bongenusa literally means honoring a king, and it may be best understood here as praying for the eternal life of King Seongjong.

In 1939, a fire destroyed many of the temple buildings. Other temple parts were destroyed in the Korean War. One of the halls that escaped the destruction houses woodblock carvings of the Flower Garland Sutra, which was finished by the monk Young-ki in 1855. There have been many renovations and repairs to the temple, and it is a thriving complex again, today, with reconstruction continuing.

Myeongdong Cathedral

This cathedral is also known as the Cathedral Church of the Virgin Mary of the Immaculate Conception. It serves Seoul's Roman Catholic Archdiocese. It is found in Jung-gu, and it is the highest prelate in the Roman Catholic religion in South Korea.

Our Lady of the Immaculate Conception is the patron saint of the Korean people, and the country of Korea. The cathedral is a landmark in the community, as well. It is an early and notable example of the revival of Korean Gothic architecture.

63 Building

The 63 Building tops out at 866 feet, and it is the tallest and most easily recognized building in Korea. It offers fantastic views of the Gwanaksan Mountains and the Hangang River.

There has been considerable renovation of 63 Building in recent years. In the basement, you'll find the largest buffet restaurant in Korea, "Buffet Pavilion", along with the 63 IMAX Theater, 63 Sea World and additional restaurants.

Children's Grand Park & Zoo

Children's Grand Park rests in 633,000 square yards of land, and is a wonderful leisure facility, especially for families. They offer performance events, amusement facilities and a botanical garden, in addition to the popular zoo.

This park and zoo opened in 1973 on Children's Day, and there are many things for youngsters to do. They include Parrot Village, Small Animal Village and the Marine Animal House, where they exhibit polar bears and seals.

Myeongdong District

This is one of the main shopping districts in Seoul. The area features mid-priced and luxury retail establishments, and outlets for international brands like Louis Vuitton, Bulgari, Forever 21, Polo Ralph Loren and Lacoste.

The area also houses cosmetics from Korea, with brands like Skin Food, The Face Shop, Missha and Nature Republic. It is quite a popular area among tourists and young people who want to sight-see and shop.

The Myeongdong Festival, run since 1982, is hosted to vitalize the area and to encourage the increase of tourism. It is generally held two times a year, one in March through April and one in September. Fashion shows, dance and music performances, parades and other events are included in the festivals. Many stores and shops offer discounts and sales during the festival times.

Seoul Night-life

Seoul is a busy city at night, with many different places to dance, socialize, eat and drink. Here are a few of the favorite night spots in Seoul.

Woodstock Music Bars

There are a few Woodstock bars in Seoul. One of the most popular is at Gangnam Station. It's a bit difficult to find, but very unique in character. The feeling is laid back and there is good music.

The Woodstock Bar takes you back to a time when vinyl records were the music of the day. You'll enjoy hearing songs you remember from years ago. This is a real bar, and the people are friendly. Travelers and expats are welcome.

3 Alley Pub

This is a large Westerner bar in European style, with beers from all over the world. 3 Alley Pub is one of the most popular and largest bars in the Itaewon area, and many expats "hang out" there often. It's a good place to catch soccer or rugby matches on TV.

They have a good menu, for a bar, serving Korean and European dishes. Weekends can get quite crowded, with expats from Australia, Europe and the US. It is often busy, but you can enjoy a drink with friends and play a game of pool.

Limelight Club

You'll find the Limelight Club across from Gecko's Terrace, near the Hamilton Hotel. It may be the hippest club of the Itaewon area, although some people consider it "shady". All you have to do is pay about $8.50 USD and grab a drink ticket. Then you can hang up your coat and start buying drinks and dancing.

The club gets crowded very late, so not many of the Americans in attendance are military members, due to their curfew. The DJ's usually play newer hip hop music and some R&B. The drinks cost between $5 and $7 each and the temperature is comfortable, even if you're dancing. The staff is friendly and caring, and help to ensure that you have an enjoyable time.

6. Special Events in Seoul, South Korea

Seollal New Year Festival

The Seollal festival is quite a celebrated event in Korea. While some Koreans celebrate the January 1st New year, most celebrate Seollal. It's a three day festival.

Seollal in 2017 will be celebrated on Saturday, January 28. Most local businesses will be closed, and residents take a few days off work to spend time with their families.

On Seollal day, people rise early in the morning and put on dressy clothes. Younger family members bow to elders, to affirm their family ties. The people offer feasts with foods that are specially prepared, including mandu-guk (dumpling soup) and tteokguk (sliced rice cake soup). Families play games like spinning tops and flying kites.

Independence Movement Day - March 1

Independence Day commemorates the South Korean Declaration of Independence. It was proclaimed in March of 1919, when the area was still colonized by Japan. There is a ceremony held each year in Seoul, at Tapgol Park, where the declaration is read.

Children's Day - May 5

On Children's day, parents dress their children and accompany them to cinemas, zoos, amusement parks or traditional parks, for lots of fun and games.

Buddha's Birthday – May 14

Buddha's birthday is marked on the 8th day of the 4th lunar month. Solemn and elaborate rituals are conducted in many temples. People hang lanterns in the courtyards as a way of celebrating the birthday of Buddha.

Memorial Day – June 6

Memorial Day honors the Korean soldiers and civilians who gave their lives for the country. A ceremony is held in Seoul, at the National Cemetery.

Liberation Day – August 15

This day is set aside to commemorate the surrender of Japan to the Allies at the end of WWII, which led to Korea's liberation in 1945.

Chuseok – September 14-16

Chuseok is among the most important traditional holidays in the year in South Korea. It is celebrated on the 15th day of the 8th lunar month. It's sometimes called Korean Thanksgiving. It celebrates the harvest, and the people give thanks for the earth's bounty. Families travel from far-flung regions of Korea, to visit the homes of their ancestors.

National Foundation Day – October 3

This is a day of commemoration of the founding of Korea by legendary god-king Dangun in 2333 BC. On Ganghwado Island, atop Manisan Mountain, a special ceremony is held on an altar that the people believe Dangun set up himself.

Christmas – December 25

This is a national holiday for Koreans, as it is for many people in other countries. Check out the huge Christmas tree by the Seoul Plaza Hotel. It creates a shine around the whole area.

The Universal Ballet in Seoul performs differing versions of The Nutcracker during the Christmas season, and they have been doing so since 1986. You can catch the show nearly every day up until January 31st.

Perhaps you would enjoy the Lotte World's Christmas Festival. It includes Santa Claus in a Christmas parade, along with other characters of the Christmas season. Songs and dancing spread good cheer.

Other Festivals & Events

Bosinggak Bell Ringing Ceremony

This historical activity takes place at the Deoksugung Palace. It started in 2006 and it occurs at noon each day. The bell is struck at least 12 times, as a signal that it is noon.

Locals sign up if they want to ring the bell, but as a tourist, you can ring it at the noontime hour any day, except on Monday, as long as you're there by 11:40 AM at the bell tower.

Hi! Seoul Festival

The Hi! Seoul Festival occurs seasonally, in winter, spring, summer and autumn. It was based upon the old "Seoul Citizens' Day" that has been held since 1994 in October, to commemorate the 600 years that Seoul has been South Korea's capital.

The festival includes many booths, where people sell clothing, foods and other items from their own countries. Cultural and Korean booths allow you to experience making traditional Korean recipes.

Seoul Performing Arts Festival

This festival is held in October each year at the Daehangno Arts Theater and the Arko Arts Theater, to create performance arts at a world-class level all in one place.

The festival includes:

- Speaking with the artists
- Seoul Dance Connection & Collection
- Interesting workshops

7. Safety in Seoul

Seoul is the 5th largest city world-wide, and even with its high population, it still retains a low crime rate, as reported by the UK Foreign & Commonwealth Office. Simply take a few precautions to make your travel in Seoul safer.

In Seoul, crimes like purse snatching, pick-pocketing and assault do occur. Private residences and hotel rooms may be burglarized. In the night club areas, rapes sometimes occur after dark. Women should not frequent these areas alone.

When you travel, secure your valuables, especially in the busy marketplaces. You can use the safe at your hotel to store your valuables while you're out. When you're in Seoul, only use public transportation and legitimate taxi cabs. Do not take riders from people in unmarked vehicles.

With the uptick in worldwide terror attacks, the US State Department advises that you remain always vigilant, especially in busy areas of the city. Public transport and areas of tourist infrastructure may be targeted for attacks. Watch for and report anything suspicious. This information is not intended to worry you. Just report anything that looks suspicious to you.

If there is some type of emergency, and you are in danger, call 112 to reach the police or 119 for the fire department or an ambulance. The US Embassy is located at 188 Sejong-daero, Jongno-gu and is open daily from 9 am to 5 pm. Phone: +82 2-397-4114.

When travelling in Seoul, don't drink tap water. Drink bottled water, instead. Many hotels serve complimentary bottled water. In general, the water is safe for drinking, but you don't want a gastro-intestinal problem to ruin your few days in Seoul.

8. Conclusion

Seoul is so much more than a technology-obsessed community. The people in South Korea are friendly, and they usually welcome strangers. Their culture emphasizes the importance of their families, and respect for other people. These customs create a comfortable bond between Koreans and visitors.

Koreans live hard. They work hard and they play hard. They do their best at everything, and customer service and tourism jobs are no exception. When you dine in Korea, you can be relatively assured of fresh foods. Most are grown locally.

Seoul may seem to be years ahead of everyone else when it comes to technology. They use neon lights, so the streets are never dark at night. The hotel rooms usually have big-screen Samsung TVs. Top of the line tech products like cell phones and computers are everywhere you look. There are even high-tech cars you'll see in Seoul, produced by Samsung.

Seoul is not as cheap as some Asian destinations, but overall, you can travel well without spending a lot of money there. Budget-minded travelers and backpackers stay in Seoul when they are touring Asia. The food is especially affordable. Street vendors are very cheap, but there are plenty of inexpensive sit-down restaurants, too.

Plan your trip well ahead of time, and look into the places you want to see before you get to Seoul. In a trip that only allows three days in town, you won't want to waste any time. Do take a little time to relax and soak in the culture, though. It's refreshing and respectful.

16163804R00028

Printed in Great Britain
by Amazon